Teacher's Handbook Of
INSTANT ACTIVITIES
...while waiting for the bell to ring

Ruth Beechick

ACCENT BOOKS
Denver, Colorado

A division of Accent Publications, Inc.
12100 W. Sixth Avenue
P.O. Box 15337
Denver, Colorado 80215

Library of Congress Catalog Card Number 79-53445

ISBN 0-89636-032-6

Here's the answer to your problem
of what to do with those few spare
minutes that happen from time to time in
your class or club or children's church
session.

You need nothing else . . .
only this book. The activities suggested
here require no advance preparation and
no special equipment.

Just pick up the book . . .
choose the activity, and do it. It's as
simple as that. Your children will have fun
and learn all at the same time. And you
will have the satisfaction of knowing that
the spare moments were not wasted.

Contents

Bible Learning Games

Find the Mistake
Head and Hips
Motion Spelling
Number, Please
Person, Place or Thing
Picture Study Game
Probe
Read 'n Think
Riddles
Secret Word
Sentence Relay
Talking Time
Team Password
Think Fast
Who Am I?
Who Did It?

Find the Mistake

After a lesson or a Bible reading try this thinking and listening game. The teacher or leader makes a statement about the lesson, but he puts a mistake in it. The one who finds the mistake gets to make the next statement.

Variations: With some groups it may work best for the teacher to make all the statements and the children to find the mistakes. The group may be divided into teams and take turns finding the mistakes. A point is earned for each error found.

Date used _____

Group_____

Response _____

Head and Hips

Players arrange in a circle if possible. A leader goes to the center, spins around with eyes closed, stops suddenly, opens his eyes and puts his hand either on his hips or on his head. If he puts his hands on his head, the player he is facing must immediately name a character in the New Testament, and if he puts his hands on his hips the player must name a character in the Old Testament. If the player is correct he gets to be leader, and if he is not correct the leader gets another turn.

Variations: If a circle is not possible the leader may spin around with eyes open, then point to a player with one hand and place the other hand on head or hips.

The responses can be changed to fit any lessons. For example, name:

a city
a body of water
a disciple

11

    a prophet
    a tribe of Israel
    a heathen nation

The game can be made more difficult by having three actions.
For example:
    hands on head for a commandment
    hands on hips for a beatitude
    hands on shoulders for a part of the Christian's armor

This game is also good for getting better acquainted.
The responses can be:
    first name
    last name
    street or subdivision
    school

Still another variation is to reverse roles. The teacher or leader names the Bible character, and all the players put their hands on head or hips to show whether it is New Testament or Old Testament. This version is more active and can be used when physical activity is needed.

Date used _____

Group_____

Response _____

Motion Spelling

A leader assigns an action to each of two letters in the alphabet. For example he may say, "For *e* you raise both hands and for *j* you stamp your foot." Everyone practices the actions briefly. Then the leader or teacher calls out a spelling word to the first player. The player spells it aloud, except for the motion letters that may be in it. For these letters he does the assigned action. If the player misses, he sits down. If he succeeds he becomes the new leader and gets to assign an action to a third letter. Players practice all three actions. A new spelling word is given to the next player. Each new leader adds another action, up to a limit of six actions.

Variations: For large groups, form two teams and score a point for every word done correctly. Alternate turns between the two teams. Leaders and new actions are added from either team, according to the successes.

For small groups (under 12) this can proceed as a spelldown. Everyone stands to begin, any player who misses sits down, and the last player to remain standing is the winner.

Word lists can be related to your lesson. The players can help you make a list by calling out words from the lesson, as you write them down. If you have a chalkboard the words can be written there for all to see. On a new, hard list players can do the motion spelling while looking at the words. When the list is more familiar, the player whose turn it is can stand with his back to the chalkboard while a word is called for him.

Make the game easier by limiting the length of the words to five or six letters. Make it harder by using longer words.

Five-letter words	Six-letter words	Longer words
Bible	Joshua	tabernacle
Jesus	priest	Pharisee
Moses	Exodus	disciple
cross	Red Sea	Calvary
angel	Jordan	Galilee
David	Israel	Bethlehem
flood	temple	shepherd
Judah	heaven	Jerusalem
Psalm	manger	Nazareth
altar	Joseph	baptize

Date used _____

Group_____

Response _____

Simple Motion Spelling: With young children it is an effective learning device to print in the air. If you have a chalkboard, print on it a word you want the children to learn—easy ones like *God* and *Bible,* or more difficult ones. Turn so you face the same direction as the children. Then you all write with your fingers in the air, and say the letters together—*G, o, d.* This works even without a chalkboard.

After your children know some words, try "back spelling." A volunteer comes to the front and you trace on his back each letter, in turn, of a word while all the children silently watch. The volunteer tries to guess the word. If he cannot, one of the watchers may be able to.

Date used _____

Group_____

Response _____

Vowel Spelling: Have a spelling contest in which contestants spell the words as usual except for the vowels. These motions are used.

> A—raise hand
> E—pull ear
> I—point to eye
> O—point to mouth
> U—point finger (you)

For younger players you may want to use actions for only one or two vowels at first.

Date used _____

Group_____

Response _____

Number, Please

Divide the group into two teams. A player on Team 1 begins by asking a player from Team 2 a question concerning numbers. The Team 2 player responds with an answer from the Bible and then proceeds to ask a question of a player on Team 1.

The exchange will proceed as in this sample.

TEAM 1: What number do you think of when I say "houses"?

TEAM 2: Two. One house was built on sand and one on the rock. What number do you think of when I say "grave"?

TEAM 1: Three. Jesus was in the grave three days and three nights.

or

Four. Lazarus was dead four days when Jesus raised him from the grave.

A team scores a point for each correct answer and loses a point for each failure to respond. But if a questioner cannot give a correct answer for his question, the one who failed to respond earns his point anyway.

Teaching suggestion: Make the game easier by allowing any team member to respond. Make it more difficult by taking turns in order, or by having the questioner call a particular player on the opposite team to answer his question.

Date used _____

Group_____

Response _____

Person, Place or Thing

One player thinks of something from the lesson the group has just had. He says, "I am thinking of something from the lesson, and it's a person (or place, or thing, or animal)."

The other players take turns trying to identify it by asking questions that are answered only by "yes" or "no."

As long as the answer is "yes" the same child continues questioning.

When the answer is "no" the next child has a turn.

When someone guesses correctly he thinks of something from the lesson and starts the game again.

Teaching suggestions: After the children have some experience with this game, give guidance about asking general questions at first. "Is it a man?" is better than asking "Is it Lot?" for an opening question. With younger children, have them whisper the item to you so you can monitor whether the questions are answered correctly.

Variation: Older children can play this as a team game. One team chooses the item. In order to win, the other team must guess it before all their team members have used up their turns. If they lose, the same team chooses the item again.

Date used _____

Group_____

Response _____

Picture Study Game

One player is chosen as leader, and the other players form two teams. The leader holds up a picture and counts to one hundred silently as all players study the picture. Then he turns the picture away from the players so that only he may see it.

The first player on Team A asks a question about the picture of the first player on Team B.

To win a point the player must correctly answer the question or correctly state that the picture does not answer it.

If he cannot answer he wins no point. If he answers something that is not shown in the picture he loses a point. The leader is the judge in all these matters.

The first Team B player next asks a question of his opponent.

Then the second players ask each other questions, and so on until everyone has had a turn.

If a player cannot ask a question, or cannot give an answer, no point is earned, but the leader gives everyone another look at the picture while he silently counts to three.

The team with the most points wins.

Teaching suggestion: Make the game easier for younger children by letting any team member ask a question or answer it, instead of taking turns in order.

Date used _____

Group_____

Response _____

Probe

Choose a familiar Bible word, such as "salvation," and indicate its letters on a chalkboard like this.

— — — — — — — — —

Or use a phrase or sentence, such as "The Lord is my shepherd."

— — — — — — — — — — — — — — — — — —

The first player guesses a letter of the alphabet. If your word contains that letter you write it in. The player gets 10 points and another turn. When he misses, the next player takes a turn. When a word is guessed, put up a new word and begin with the next player. Each player keeps track of his own points.

Do not fill in two letters at a time. For instance, if someone guesses *A* and your word is *salvation* you fill in only one of the *A*'s for that guess.

Suggested words to use:

angel	faith	Jew
baptize	forgive	justification
believe	Gentile	prophet
Bible	gospel	revelation
Creator	grace	righteousness
eternity	Heaven	Savior

Suggested sentences to use:

In the beginning God created the heaven and the earth.

Thou shalt have no other gods before me.

Thou shalt not kill.

Thou shalt not steal.

O Lord our Lord, how excellent is thy name in all the earth.

The heavens declare the glory of God.

Thy word is a lamp unto my feet.

Create in me a clean heart.

Ye shall find the babe wrapped in swaddling clothes, lying in a manger.

Blessed are the pure in heart: for they shall see God.

For all have sinned and come short of the glory of God.

For whosoever shall call upon the name of the Lord shall be saved.

Date used _____

Group_____

Response _____

Variations. You can give a bonus of 50 points for finishing a word or phrase. You can also add the "I got it" feature. Any player who thinks he knows the answer may interrupt by raising his hand and saying "I got it." After you recognize him, he makes his guess. If he is right he gains the 50 points, but if he is wrong he subtracts 50 points. "I got it" can only be called when there are at least five spaces still blank.

Date used _____

Group_____

Response _____

Read 'n Think

Use a Bible or Bible story book at a suitable reading level for the players. One player comes to the front, chooses a sentence from the book and reads the first word. Other players all try to guess the second word. If no one does, the reader begins the sentence again and reads two words. Others guess again. Play continues in this manner until someone guesses the correct next word. This guesser becomes the new reader. He chooses another sentence, not the following one, and play begins again.

Here is an example of how the game will proceed:

READER: The . . .

GROUP: Law. Israelites. King.

READER: The Lord . . .

GROUP: Said. Loveth.

READER: The Lord is . . .

GROUP: Good. My.

READER: That's right. The Lord is my shepherd.

Date used _____

Group_____

Response _____

Riddles

This game is immensely popular with children who have recently learned to handle riddles and they like to repeat it week after week. It consists simply of taking turns making up riddles and presenting them to the rest of the group. A sample riddle is:

> This man obeyed God.
> He built a boat.
> Who is he?

Riddles may be about persons, places, animals or objects. Whoever guesses the answer may take the next turn giving a riddle. But if he does not have one ready he may choose a volunteer to give a riddle for him.

Date used _____

Group_____

Response _____

Secret Word

A volunteer who has a secret word ready is chosen to be the first leader. The secret word should be a familiar word from the Bible—either a proper or common noun.

Players begin asking the leader questions which can be answered "yes" or "no." Examples:

Is it a person?
Is it a place?
Did Jesus go there?
Do we read about it in the Old Testament?

For each yes answer the leader must tell one letter in his word. He tells the letters in a scrambled order, and double letters are revealed separately. The leader tells the group when all the letters are given. At this time the players make five guesses. The one who guesses correctly becomes the new leader. If no one guesses within five tries the same leader remains for another round.

Teaching suggestions: Players may keep track of letters individually with pencil and paper, or one child may write them on the chalkboard. The leader should have his word written down, and should mark off letters as he tells them.

Date used _____

Group_____

Response _____

Sentence Relay

Divide the group into two or more teams. The object of the relay is to write a sentence about the lesson just completed.

The first player on each team runs to the board and writes a word, then dashes back and hands the chalk to the player next in line.

The second player writes a word either before or after the first one.

Each player in turn must add a word to the sentence but must avoid completing it before the last teammate's turn.

The last player writes a word that completes the sentence, and he also puts in any capitalization and punctuation needed.

The team that finishes first with a complete sentence scores.

Date used _____

Group_____

Response _____

Talking Time

The players all divide into pairs. Each pair chooses two Bible characters to be. They might be:

Jonathan and David
Jacob and Isaac
Jacob and Esau
Jacob and Rebekah
or any two people who could have talked together.

They plan a conversation about an actual Bible incident. After the planning time one pair gives their conversation, which should be limited to a minute or two. They should be careful never to mention each other's names.

After time is called the other players guess who they are and what the situation is.

The player who guesses correctly goes up with his partner for the next conversation.

Date used _____

Group_____

Response _____

Team Password

Divide the group into two teams. One member from each team comes to the front and you whisper the password to both of them, or show it to them on a slip of paper. The password may be any Bible word, such as Adam, Abraham, tomb, tabernacle or salvation.

The players in front take turns giving one-word clues to their teams. After each clue the team tries to guess the word.

Guessing can proceed in the way that best seems to fit the size group you have. Either take turns, or the clue-giver chooses someone whose hand is raised, or take all guesses that are given within five seconds of the clue.

A team earns ten points if they guess the password after one clue, nine points after the second clue, and so on.

Date used _____

Group_____

Response _____

Think Fast

A leader faces the other players. He suddenly calls "Genesis" or any Bible book, points to a player, and begins counting to 20.

The player must give a fact about Genesis before the leader reaches 20. He may say, "The first book," or "It tells about Adam and Eve," or anything true about the book.

If he fails to answer in time he becomes the leader. Any book may be repeated, but the same facts cannot be used twice.

Variations: (1) If a player thinks the leader has called a book that the leader himself knows nothing about, he may choose not to answer and instead call "Challenge." At this call he points to the leader and begins counting to 20 himself. If the leader fails he continues to be *It,* but if he names a fact the challenging player becomes leader.

(2) Use names of Bible characters instead of Bible books.

Date used _____

Group_____

Response _____

Who Am I?

One player is a Bible person. He is a volunteer who has written down the name of a Bible person and three words closely related to the person. For instance, he might write "Joshua: Jordan River, Jericho, spy."

A questioner is chosen, who comes to the front with the Bible person. The questioner looks at the name and the list of words. He asks questions intended to help the other players guess who the person is, but he cannot use any of the words on the list. For instance, he can ask, "Did the water stop flowing and make a path for you?" but he cannot ask, "Did you cross the Jordan River on dry land?"

When someone guesses, he can become the next Bible person, or if he is not ready he can choose someone to take his place. The questioner chooses someone to take his place as next questioner.

Teaching suggestions: The game can be made more difficult by listing five words that cannot be used in the questioning, instead of three. The Bible person should try to select words that will make it difficult for the questioner to succeed.

Date used _____

Group_____

Response _____

Who Did It?

The teacher or a leader begins this game by asking the identity of a character from a particular story. Some sample questions are:

Who kept digging more wells?
Who consented to Stephen's death?
Who hung a red cord from her window?

The first player who names the character gets to tell more about the story and then ask the next question.

Date used _____

Group_____

Response _____

Bible Book Drills

Name Six
What's Next?
Zip

Name Six

This is a "Hot Potato" game with many possible variations. In its circle form *It* is in the center and closes his eyes while those in the circle pass around the hot potato. Any handy object will do for the potato. When *It* claps his hands the player with the object must keep it. *It* then names a book of the Bible. The player with the object begins to pass it around the circle again, at the same time naming the Bible book and the five following books—six in all. He must complete the naming before the object comes back to him, or he becomes *It.*

Variations: If the players are seated in rows, you could agree on a certain path for the object to travel during the naming of six books. For instance, it could go to the end of the row, down the next row, back to the original row and up to the player who started it. This makes a small circle out of two rows.

A more active version is to agree on an exercise to do while naming the books—six toe touches, six deep knee bends, six turn-arounds on one foot, and so forth. All the players may do the exercises, or only a few volunteers. They sit down after the six exercises. The leader must judge whether the books are named correctly and whether they are named before all the exercisers sit down.

Date used _____

Group_____

Response _____

What's Next?

All players stand. The leader chooses one player to begin reciting the books of the Bible. As soon as the leader taps that player on the head and points to a second player, the first stops reciting and the second continues from where he left off. The leader soon taps the second player and a third player continues. Any player who misses must sit down. The last player(s) standing is the winner.

Variation: Instead of the leader choosing players at random, play may proceed around a circle or up and down rows of seats. The game is easier this way and could be introduced in this form, and the more difficult form used after the players are familiar with the game and do it well.

Date used _____

Group_____

Response _____

Zip

Any book from the New Testament is *zip,* and any book from the Old Testament is *zip-zip. It* names a book, points to a player, and begins counting to five softly. The player must answer either *zip* or *zip-zip* as the case may be before the count of five. *It* continues calling books and pointing until some player answers incorrectly or too late. That player then becomes *It.*

Variations: Any two categories can be used. Some possibilities are:

>   disciples and non-disciples
>   prophets and kings
>   fruit of the Spirit and fruit of the flesh

Date used _____

Group_____

Response _____

Simply-for-Fun Games

Challenge
Clown
Discover the Rules
Follow the Leader
Mimic

Challenge

Use an object handy to your room, such as a chalkboard eraser or paper cup. Form two teams. The first player on Team A asks his partner on Team B if he can perform a particular action with the eraser balanced on some part of his body, for example, "Can you turn around three times with the eraser on your toes?"

The player on Team B may say "Yes," perform the challenge and gain a point for his team. But if he says "Yes" and fails to perform it Team A gets the point.

Or the Team B player may say "No." In this case the challenger may let his opponent have the point by agreeing that it is impossible, or he may perform the feat himself and gain a point for his own team.

When this challenge is completed, the two players reverse positions, with the Team B player becoming the challenger. Next, the second players on each team come up and everyone watches their challenges to each other.

Date used _____

Group_____

Response _____

Clown

The first player thinks of a word and gives the first letter. Each following player adds a letter which will form a word but not finish it. Anyone who finishes a word is one-third of a clown. Then the next player starts a new word.

For older children, you may say that the first three letters do not count. For instance, if the first two letters are F and O, a player may add R without being penalized, as the word may go on to become FORGOT or FORGIVE or something else.

If a player cannot think of a word, he may bluff and name a letter which might help form a word. However, he may be challenged. Any player on his turn may challenge the player preceding him, and if that player cannot name a word which could be formed from the letters given he becomes one-third of a clown.

Variation: Clowns are out of the game. But they can add much fun by talking to players and trying to get them to reply. Any player who slips and replies to a clown adds one-third of a clown to his score.

Date used _____

Group_____

Response _____

Discover the Rules

The teacher or leader decides on rules for answering yes and no questions. For instance, if a question ends with letters A through M answer "Yes," and if it ends with N through Z answer "No." All players begin asking yes or no questions and the leader answers according to his rules. The first person to discover the rules wins.

Let winners or volunteers become leaders whenever they can think up their own rules.

Date used _____

Group_____

Response _____

Follow the Leader

For a classroom version of this game everyone stays "in place" and follows the action of the leader. Teacher can be leader for a while, and then volunteers who have ideas may lead their ideas. The game can be physical, verbal, or musical. Following are some ideas for the leader to use.

Physical. Do each of these in place, and continue for half a minute or so on each action.
hopping
skipping
running
deep knee bends
toe touches

Verbal
   Spell a Bible word.
   Recite the books of the New Testament or Old
      Testament.
   Recite a memory verse.

Musical
   Sing a chorus.
   Sing a hymn.
   Clap the rhythm of a familiar song.

Date used _____

Group_____

Response _____

Mimic

One player is chosen to be *It* and he leaves the room. The remaining players choose a leader, perform whatever actions the leader performs, while trying not to look at him and give away his identity.

It is called back into the room. He gets three guesses to find the leader. If he succeeds the leader becomes the new *It* and if he does not succeed he is *It* for another time.

Date used _____

Group_____

Response _____

Brain Teasers

At the Well
Belshazzar's Guests
Boaz the Farmer
Daniel's Friends
Digging in Jerusalem
Esau the Hunter
Gideon the Farmer
Isaac
Job's Family
Joseph's Brothers
Joseph the Carpenter
Peter the Fisherman
Superstitious Kings
The Oldest Man

At the Well

Rebekah went to the well with a five-log jar and a three-log jar. She was told to bring back exactly seven logs of water. How did she do it? (A log is a bit less than a pint in our measures.)

Answer: She filled the five-log jar, filled the three-log jar from it, and then poured the three logs onto the ground. She poured the remaining two logs into the smaller jar and refilled the five-log jar, giving her seven logs.

Date used _____

Group_____

Response _____

Rachel went to the well with the same size jars—a five-log and a three-log. She was told to bring back exactly four logs of water. How did she do it?

Answer: She filled the three-log jar and poured it into the five-log. She filled the three-log jar a second time and poured as much as she could into the larger jar. This left her with one log in the smaller jar. She emptied the large jar and poured her one log into it. Then she refilled the three-log jar, and had exactly four logs.

Date used _____

Group_____

Response _____

Belshazzar's Guests

Belshazzar the king made a great feast. We do not know who attended the feast, but let's say that four of the men were Nebai, Iddo, Ono and Lod. Can you seat these men in their proper order? Here are the clues.

Nebai was not at the end and he was not next to Iddo. Ono sat at the left of the man who sat at the left of Lod.

Teaching suggestions: Puzzles of this kind take time to work out. Children who have poor problem solving skills often ask for the answer right away, while those with good thinking skills prefer the challenge of working it out. You might help the former and recognize the work of the latter by letting the children work as a group. They can share ideas and clues, they can test out each other's suggestions, and so forth. Exposures to this "thinking out loud" will help many of your children to become better thinkers.

Answer: When you are facing the men they will appear in this order: Lod, Nebai, Ono, Iddo.

Date used _____

Group_____

Response _____

Boaz the Farmer

Boaz was a farmer and this teaser could have been about him. A farmer had 3 5/6 haystacks in one field and 5 1/7 haystacks in another field. He put them all together. How many did he have then?

Answer: Only one stack, of course.

Date used _____

Group_____

Response _____

Boaz the farmer had seventeen sheep. All but nine broke through the fence and wandered away. How many were left?

Answer: Nine.

Date used _____

Group_____

Response _____

Daniel's Friends

Shadrach, Meshach and Abed-nego were good friends in Daniel's time. Let's pretend they were the ones who got their clothes mixed up after a visit one evening. See if you can figure out who took Shadrach's turban. Here are the clues.

Each friend took the cloak of one man and the turban of another, and no man had his own. Abed-nego took Meshach's turban.

Answer: (Don't give this answer too soon. It would be more fun to let your children take this puzzle home and work on it all week.) Meshach is the one who took Shadrach's turban—and Abed-nego's cloak. Here are the others. Shadrach took Abed-nego's turban and Meshach's cloak. Abed-nego took Meshach's turban and Shadrach's cloak.

Date used _____

Group_____

Response _____

Digging in Jerusalem

Suppose you were to start boring a hole exactly through the earth, starting from Jerusalem. Where would you come out?

Answer: Where you went in.

Date used _____

Group_____

Response _____

Esau the Hunter

Esau was a hunter and this story could have been about him. One day a hunter's bow wasn't working properly and he took aim at some crows on a log. Half the crows flew away but one returned immediately. The hunter shot again, and again half the crows flew away and one returned.

On counting the crows now, he found that there were exactly the same number of crows on the log as there were at first.

How many were on the log originally?

Answer: There were two crows on the log originally.

Date used _____

Group_____

Response _____

Gideon the Farmer

Where did farmer Gideon get two eggs for breakfast every morning if he had no chickens and no one gave him any eggs and he did not beg, borrow or steal any eggs?

Answer: From his ducks. Or his geese.

Date used _____

Group_____

Response _____

Let's say Gideon could thresh a basket of grain in 2 hours, but it took his son 3 hours to do the same job. If they worked together how long would it take to thresh a basket of grain?

Answer: One hour and 12 minutes. In 1 hour Gideon filled 1/2 basket and his son 1/3 basket. This is 5/6 per hour. It would take 1/5 hour to do the last 1/6.

Date used _____

Group_____

Response _____

If Gideon ran into his field to get away from the Midianites, how far into the field could he go?

Answer: Half way. After that he would be coming out.

Date used _____

Group_____

Response _____

Isaac

Isaac could only make a success of his work by starting at the top and working down. What was his work?

Answer: Digging wells.

Date used _____

Group_____

Response _____

Isaac had twin sons. Here is a puzzle about them.
"My name is Jacob," said the twin with red hair.
"My name is Esau," said the twin with black hair.
If at least one twin was lying, which boy had red hair and which had black hair?

Answer: Esau had red hair and Jacob had black hair. If one twin was lying the other could not be telling the truth either, or you would end up with the result that both have the same color hair. Thus both must have been lying, so switch their statements around and see who had red hair and who had black.

Date used _____

Group_____

Response _____

Job's Family

How many sons and daughters were in Job's family? Here are the clues.

Each brother had twice as many brothers as sisters, but each sister has only two sisters.

Answer: Seven sons and three daughters (Job 1:2).

Date used _____

Group_____

Response _____

Job lost his first family of children but God gave him another. In this latter family each brother had six other brothers and the total of children was ten. How many sons and daughters were in Job's latter family?

Answer: Seven sons and three daughters (Job 42:13).

Date used _____

Group_____

Response _____

Joseph's Brothers

If Reuben carried a bag of grain and Simeon carried three bags the size of Reuben's, how can it be that Reuben's load was heavier?

Answer: Simeon's bags were empty.

Date used _____

Group_____

Response _____

Joseph and his brothers were twelve sons of one father. Each son had one sister. How many children were in this large family?

Answer: Thirteen.

Date used _____

Group_____

Response _____

Joseph the Carpenter

If carpenter Joseph received one coin for sawing a board into two lengths, how much did he receive for sawing a board into four lengths?

Answer: Three coins.

Date used _____

Group_____

Response _____

Peter the Fisherman

One day Peter caught a very large fish. It weighed ten manehs plus one-half of its total weight. How heavy was Peter's fish?

Answer: Twenty manehs.

Date used _____

Group_____

Response _____

Superstitious Kings

Ancient kings were often superstitious about certain numbers. A story (probably a make-believe one) says that such a king asked for 24 lambs to be brought for a feast. He commanded that the lambs be brought alive in four pens and there must be an odd number of lambs in each pen. If you were the servant how would you manage to obey this command?

Answer: Seven lambs in each of three pens and a fourth pen surrounding the other three. Or the lambs in the first three pens may distributed in some other way, such as five, seven, nine.

Date used _____

Group_____

Response _____

This same king had a criminal to execute and he wanted to give the criminal a choice of how he should die. "Make one statement," the king said. "If your statement is true you will be hanged and if it is false you will be thrown to the lions." After the criminal's statement, the king had to set him free. What did the man say?

Answer: "I'll be thrown to the lions." He was only to be hanged if his statement was true, but hanging would make the statement false. He was only to be thrown to the lions if his statement was false, but this death would make the statement true. So the king could not execute him either way, and he set him free.

Date used _____

Group_____

Response _____

Here is another story about an ancient king. The king did not like it when one of his officers fell in love with his beautiful daughter. He decided to call the officer to a drawing. Two broken pieces of pottery would be put into a vase. If the officer drew one with his beloved's name on it, he could marry her that very day. But if he drew a blank one he would be banished from the kingdom forever.

As the officer approached the throne room he overheard the king say to his queen, "Do not fear. I have made both pieces blank."

But the officer married the princess that day. How did he manage it?

Answer: He drew one piece of pottery and crushed it under his foot. Then he asked that the remaining piece be shown to the witnesses. Of course it was blank.

Date used _____

Group_____

Response _____

The Oldest Man

Methuselah was the oldest man who ever lived, yet he died before his father. How can that be?

Answer: His father was Enoch who walked with God and did not die.

Date used _____

Group_____

Response _____

Start with the number 1 and use only whole numbers. Do you use the letter *a* in spelling a number before you get to Methuselah's age?

Answer: No. Methuselah died at 969, and you do not use a until one thousand.

Date used _____

Group_____

Response _____

Mental Arithmetic

Do In Your Head

(Read slowly.)

Take the number of days of creation, multiply by 11.

6 x 11 = 66 (books in the Bible)

Take the number of books in the Bible, subtract the number of books in the New Testament.

66 − 27 = 39 (books in the Old Testament)

Take the number of books in the Old Testament, multiply the first digit by the second digit.

3 x 9 = 27 (books in the New Testament)

Take the number of the tribes of Israel, multiply by itself, multiply by 1000.

12 x 12 x 1000 = 144,000 (servants of God in Revelation 7)

Take the number of the books of Moses, add the number of commandments, subtract the days of creation, add the number of true Gods, divide by the number of tablets God wrote the commandments on.

5 + 10 − 6 + 1 ÷ 2 = 5 (books of Moses, where you can read all these things)

Take the number of years Moses lived in Egypt, add the number of years he lived in the desert, add the years of wandering in the wilderness.

40 + 40 + 40 = 120 (age of Moses when he died)

After Job's troubles were over God blessed him with twice as much wealth as before. Here is a list of what Job had before his troubles. Tell what God gave him later.

Before	*After*
7000 sheep	*14,000*
3000 camels	*6000*
500 yoke (teams) of oxen	*1000*
500 female donkeys	*1000*

Gideon has 32,000 men. Twenty-two thousand were afraid and went home, so how many did he have then? (10,000) Nine thousand seven hundred of these were rejected because they bowed on their knees to drink. How many were left then?

300 (Gideon won his battle with these men.)

God the Father is one person, Jesus the Son is one person, the Holy Spirit is one person. Multiply 1 times 1 times 1 and what do you have?

1 x 1 x 1 = 1 (God)

The king of Samaria sent a captain of fifty with his fifty to get Elijah. Elijah called down fire from heaven to consume them. Again the king sent a captain of fifty with his fifty and again Elijah called down fire from heaven to consume them. A third time the king sent a captain of fifty with his fifty, and this time Elijah went with them to the king. How many men died?

102 (I Kings 1:9-15)

Music and Rhythm

Do, Re, Mi
Guess the Song
Rhythm Mime
Simonson Plays
Orchestra

Do, Re, Mi

Begin by having the total group practice singing the scale. Then select eight children to line up and represent the eight notes. Point to the "notes" one at a time and have them sing. When they can go up and down the scale okay, try various jumps. Try a tune. Let other children try to play tunes on the scale. Play this one and see who recognizes the tune.

```
sol  mi  mi  re  mi  sol  sol
la   la  do  la  la  sol  sol
sol  mi  mi  re  mi  sol  sol
la   la  sol do      mi  re  do
```

Date used _____

Group_____

Response _____

Guess the Song

One player claps out the rhythm of a song familiar to the group. The first person to guess the song claps out the next song.

Variations: (1) The clapper can use pencils or a simple percussion instrument if any is available.

(2) Children age nine or over may play this game with two teams, or rhythm bands. One band agrees on a song and claps or plays it with percussion instruments for the other players to guess.

Date used _____

Group_____

Response _____

Rhythm Mime

It claps a rhythm, and then points to a player to reproduce the rhythm. If the player is correct *It* points to other players one at a time to reproduce the rhythm. The first to miss becomes *It.* Or if no one misses, *It* plays another rhythm, trying to make it more complicated than the first.

Variation: Rhythm instruments may be used if they are available.

Date used _____

Group_____

Response _____

Simonson Plays

A leader has two ways to make rhythm, such as tapping on the table and tapping a foot on the floor. If instruments are available the two ways may be to strike a piano key or strike a tone bell. One of the instruments is labeled Simonson. Every time Simonson plays a rhythm the players reproduce it by clapping. When the other instrument plays, no one else should either.

The leader should play his rhythms in quick succession and try to make players miss. Anyone who does is out until a new game is started with a new leader.

Date used _____

Group_____

Response _____

Orchestra

All players are assigned to an orchestra section—violins, cellos, flutes, drums, and so forth. Use fewer sections for younger children and more sections for older children.

A conductor begins singing a song and at the same time pantomiming the playing of one of the orchestra instruments. All orchestra members pantomime playing their own instruments. When the conductor switches instruments that is the signal for those who play that instrument to switch to the one the conductor just quit using. When the conductor switches again, that section resumes their own instruments and the next section must switch. For instance, the conductor begins by playing a drum. He switches to flute. At that signal the flute players begin playing drums. Next, the conductor switches to violin. The violinists now switch to flute—the instrument the conductor just quit—and the flute players resume their own instrument.

Date used _____

Group_____

Response _____

Discussions

Moral Behavior Discussions
One-Verse Discussions
    Beginnings
    Endings
    Heaven
    Hell
    Salvation

Moral Behavior Discussions

Jason is playing a game with his little brother Mike. Mike doesn't understand the rules very well so Jason could easily work things out so that he wins any time he wants to. Mike has fun anyway. How do you think Jason should play the game?

Date used _____

Group_____

Response _____

Jenny was standing in line at a drinking fountain when Donna pushed her way in front. Jenny thought that was bad manners, but she just moved back a bit to make room and said nothing. Do you think Jenny should have fought for her rights? Why?

Can you think of other unfair things that sometimes happen to children? Tell about them. Read I Corinthians 6:7. See what Isaac did in Genesis 26:18-22. How do you think God wants children to act when something unfair happens?

Date used _____

Group_____

Response _____

Tommy doesn't understand arithmetic, but he doesn't want to admit it, so he pretends it's just that he doesn't like it and he makes excuses for not getting his work done. If you were Tommy's friend what would you tell Tommy? Is there any way you can help Tommy?

Date used _____

Group_____

Response _____

Dick had to report on five books. He chose one book that looked like a good adventure story. After he got into it a way and was really interested in the story he found out that it was about occultism—talking with spirits and things. What should Dick do?

Date used _____

Group_____

Response _____

Susie was at a pajama party at her girlfriend's house and the girls started to play with a Ouija board. Susie remembered learning in Sunday school that a Ouija board is of the devil. What should Susie do?

Date used _____

Group_____

Response _____

Someone in Robbie's gang of friends got a book that tells about old black magic things. After school each day the boys go to their meeting place to look at the book together. What should Robbie do?

Date used _____

Group_____

Response _____

The Lord told Solomon to ask for anything he wanted, and he asked for wisdom. If you could have anything you want, what would you ask for? Why? What would you do with it?

Date used _____

Group_____

Response _____

A group of Dale's friends were having fun trying to eat some marijuana seeds a boy brought to school. Byron knew it was harmful to smoke the grass that grows from the seeds, but he didn't know about eating the seeds. What should Byron do?

Date used _____

Group_____

Response _____

Dawn is a gentle girl and she doesn't like to fight or have trouble with people. Every once in a while a big, retarded boy named Carl traps Dawn or her friends and kisses them. They ask to go in a kind way and a stern way but he doesn't go. Carl is very strong. What should Dawn and her friends do?

Date used _____

Group_____

Response _____

Cathy and Mary are sisters. They share the same room and they usually get along pretty well with each other. But one day the room was messy, and they got into an argument about cleaning it. Cathy told Mary to hurry, and Mary said it's mostly Cathy's stuff anyway. Mary shouted and Cathy hit, and it was a big fight.

After it was over Mary felt bad and wondered if she should apologize. But then she remembered that Cathy started it, so she thought Cathy should apologize. What do you think Mary should do now?

Date used _____

Group_____

Response _____

One-Verse Discussions

Beginnings

Genesis 1:1

This is the first sentence of what story? (*Creation.*)

Close your eyes and think about this beginning. Can you make a mental picture of it? What is your picture like?

Do you think this was hard for God to do? Why or why not?

If you were writing the story of creation what would your first sentence be?

Date used _____

Group _____

Response _____

John 1:1

This is the first sentence of what story? (*Story of Jesus.*)

Jesus is the Word. What does this verse tell about Jesus?

Who was Jesus?

When was the beginning?

Where was Jesus in the beginning?

Did Jesus live with God before He was born on earth? Can you prove your answer from this verse?

How is that different from your birth?

Date used _____

Group _____

Response _____

Endings

Hebrews 1:11

What does "they" refer to? (You will have to look back one verse to find out.)

Do you see two verbs here that are opposites? What are they?

What will perish?

What will remain?

Think about a piece of your clothing which your mother threw away. Can you remember how it was when new? Did you like it? Did it get old all in one day? Or did it slowly wear out? Who wants to tell us about one of your things?

Can you see the earth wearing out like this? What do you see?

In your science books have you read of any ways the earth is wearing out? What?

Date used _____

Group_____

Response _____

II Peter 3:10

This verse tells the ending of what?

How are the heavens going to end?

How is the earth going to end?

Who has read or heard of some other way people think the world will end? Tell about it.

What day will the world end? Do we know when that day will be? Prove your answers from this verse.

If you belong to God's kingdom and not to the earth's kingdoms, how will you feel on this day? Why?

Date used _____

Group_____

Response _____

Heaven

John 14:2

Jesus is talking. So who is the Father?

What does God have where He lives?

What does Jesus say He is going to do?

Do you want one of these mansions, or homes? What do you hope it is like?

Date used _____

Group_____

Response _____

I Corinthians 2:9

What do you think are some of the things God has pre-
pared for us who love Him? (*Maybe Heaven, mansions.*)
Has anyone ever seen these things?
Has anyone ever heard these things described?
Has anyone ever imagined these things in their hearts?
When you try to imagine Heaven, what do you think of?
Will Heaven be as good as you imagine? Will it be better?
What makes you think that?

Date used _____

Group_____

Response _____

Hell

Revelation 20:10

This verse has not happened yet. John tells the future as
though it had already happened. What does this verse tell
you?
What did the devil do to people?
Where is the devil thrown?
How long does the lake of fire burn?
Do you think God will change His mind and let the devil
out some day? Would this verse be true if He did?
If you painted a picture of this verse what would you put
in your picture?

Date used _____

Group_____

Response _____

Revelation 20:15

This verse has not happened yet. John tells the future as though it already happened. What book is important here? What seems to be written in it?

What happens to people whose names are not in the book?

If everyone in the world knew about this verse what do you think they would want to do? What do you want to do?

If you painted a picture of this verse what would you put in your picture?

Date used _____

Group_____

Response _____

Salvation

Acts 4:12

This verse tells about an important name. Look back in verse 10 to see what this name is.

What is important about this name? What can Jesus Christ do for us?

Can anyone else do this? Prove your answer from the verse.

Sometimes people say, "There are many roads to Heaven, and we will all get there in our own ways." What do you think about this? What does the verse say about it?

If everyone in the world knew this verse what do you think they would want to do? What do you want to do?

Date used _____

Group_____

Response _____

Romans 10:13

Do you think this verse is hard or easy to understand? What does it tell you?

Some people think if they live pretty good and are not criminals or anything like that, they will be saved. Do you think they are right? Prove your answer from this verse.

Some people think if they belong to a Christian church they will be saved. Are they right? Prove your answer from this verse.

Can a thief be saved? Why do you answer that way? Can a murderer be saved? Can a good person be saved? Who can be saved? Who cannot be saved? Prove your answers from this verse.

Can you be saved? How?

Date used _____

Group_____

Response _____

Bible Quizzes

Quiz Games
Quiz on Jesus
Quiz on God
Quiz on Salvation
Quiz on Sons
Quiz on Sisters and Wives
Quiz on Bible Authors
Quiz on Numbers (10 or below)
Quiz on Numbers (over 10)
Quiz on When Did It Happen? Series I
Quiz on When Did It Happen? Series II
Quiz on The Old World or the New?
Quiz on Christmas
Quiz on Easter

Quiz Games

(The quizzes included in this section can be used with any of these games.)

Active Answers. This is fun for all quizzes where there are a limited number of choices, such as True—False or "Before the flood"—"After the flood." Plan a different action for each answer choice. For instance, raise the right hand for a true answer and raise the left hand for a false answer. Some other possibilities are: clapping, touching head or toes, standing, sitting, walking to touch the door. The actions can be as quiet or as active as you wish, and all the children answer at once. In quizzes with more than two choices this game still works, but it requires more concentration.

Date used _____

Group_____

Response _____

Bible Baseball. Form two teams. One team is at bat, and they score a run for each correct answer and an out for each incorrect answer. After three outs the other team comes to bat.

Date used _____

Group_____

Response _____

Bible Basketball. Form two teams. Give questions by turns to the teams. A correct answer is a basket and earns two points. An incorrect answer is a foul, which gives the opposing team a free throw (using the missed question). A successful free throw earns one point.

Date used _____

Group_____

Response _____

Tic-Tac-Toe. On the chalkboard draw a tic-tac-toe grid. Form two teams—an X team and an O team. Ask questions of each team in turn. After a player gives a correct answer he gets to place an X or O for his team. When there is a winning row begin a new game.

Date used _____

Group_____

Response _____

Church. Form two teams. For each correct answer a team gets to add a line to draw a church. The winning team is the one which first completes its church.

Date used _____

Group_____

Response _____

A variation of this is to have a teacher church and a class church. For each correct answer the class adds a line to their church, and for each incorrect answer the teacher adds a line to his church. See who first completes the church.

Date used _____

Group_____

Response _____

Two Tries. This is not exactly a game, but it is an extremely effective paper-and-pencil way to learn from quizzes. Read approximately five questions and let the children write their answers. Then read the five answers while each child checks his own work. The children turn their papers to the other side, you read the same five questions again, and the children check their answers again. The second time almost everyone will have their answers right. Those who miss will probably only miss one. See how easy it is to learn?

Date used _____

Group_____

Response _____

Jesus

1. Jesus is God's only Son. *(T)*
2. Jesus is both God and man. *(T)*
3. Jesus lived in Heaven before He came to earth. *(T)*
4. The reason Jesus came was to be a teacher. *(F)*
5. The reason Jesus came was to die for our sins. *(T)*
6. Jesus did not let people worship Him. *(F)*
7. Jesus accepted worship from people. *(T)*
8. It was God's plan for Jesus to die. *(T)*
9. Jesus' body is now in the grave. *(F)*
10. Jesus' body is raised and in Heaven. *(T)*
11. People who believe in Jesus will be raised in three days after death as He was. *(F)*
12. People who believe in Jesus will be with Him as soon as they die. *(T)*
13. Jesus will come to earth again as a baby. *(F)*
14. Jesus will come to earth again as a king. *(T)*
15. Jesus told us exactly when He will come. *(F)*
16. Jesus wants us to expect Him at any time. *(T)*

Date used _____

Group_____

Response _____

God

1. God is one God in three persons. *(T)*
2. God has no beginning and no ending. *(T)*
3. God created everything except Satan. *(F)*
4. Someday God will make other gods. *(F)*
5. God loves everyone in the world. *(T)*
6. God sent His Son Jesus into the world to save sinners. *(T)*
7. God listens to prayers of only good men. *(F)*
8. God will save sinners who seek Him. *(T)*
9. God judged the world by a flood. *(T)*
10. Someday God will judge the world by fire. *(T)*
11. God cannot be bothered with unimportant people. *(F)*
12. God has all knowledge. *(T)*
13. God has all power. *(T)*
14. God is everywhere. *(T)*
15. God sinned once a long time ago. *(F)*
16. God spoke to us through the Bible and through Jesus. *(T)*
17. Outer space is what separates us from God. *(F)*
18. Sin is what separates us from God. *(T)*

Date used _____

Group_____

Response _____

Salvation

1. God made a way for all people to be saved. *(T)*
2. All people have sinned. *(T)*
3. All people are saved through Jesus' death. *(F)*
4. To be saved we must believe on Jesus. *(T)*
5. To be saved we must repent of our sins. *(T)*
6. To be saved we must be baptized. *(F)*
7. To be saved we must go to church. *(F)*
8. Jesus is preparing a home for those who believe in Him. *(T)*
9. Hell was prepared for the devil and his angels. *(T)*
10. Only the devil and his angels will go to Hell. *(F)*
11. People who do not believe in Jesus will go to Hell. *(T)*
12. If people do not believe Jesus now there will always be more time. *(F)*
13. Jesus knows what will make us happy better than we do ourselves. *(T)*
14. The heavenly home is better than anyone can imagine. *(T)*
15. Everyone goes to the heavenly home after death. *(F)*
16. Only those who are saved go to Heaven after death. *(T)*

Date used _____

Group_____

Response _____

Sons

1. Who was the first son of Adam and Eve? *(Cain)*
2. Who was the third son of Adam and Eve? *(Seth)*
3. Who was the grandson of Methuselah? *(Noah)*
4. Who was the son of Abraham and Sarah? *(Isaac)*
5. Who were the twin sons of Isaac? *(Jacob and Esau)*
6. Who was the youngest son of Jacob? *(Benjamin)*
7. Who was called the son of Pharaoh's daughter? *(Moses)*
8. Who was the son of Nun? *(Joshua)*
9. Who was the first son of Hannah? *(Samuel)*
10. Who was the great-grandson of Ruth and Boaz? *(David)*
11. Who was the youngest son of Jesse? *(David)*
12. Who was the son of David and Bathsheba? *(Solomon)*
13. Who was the son of Zacharias and Elisabeth? *(John the Baptist)*
14. Who was the first son of Mary? *(Jesus)*
15. Who were the two sons of Zebedee? *(James and John)*
16. Who was the son of Eunice? *(Timothy)*

Date used _____

Group_____

Response _____

Sisters and Wives

1. Who was the wife of Adam? *(Eve)*
2. Who was the first wife of Abraham? *(Sarah)*
3. Who was the wife of Isaac? *(Rebekah)*
4. Who was the best-loved wife of Jacob? *(Rachel)*
5. Who was the sister of Rachel? *(Leah)*
6. Who was the sister of Jacob's twelve sons? *(Dinah)*
7. Who was the sister of Moses? *(Miriam)*
8. Who was the wife of Boaz? *(Ruth)*
9. Who was the Jewish wife of King Ahasuerus? *(Esther)*
10. Who was the wife of Ahab? *(Jezebel)*
11. Who were the sisters of Lazarus? *(Mary and Martha)*
12. Who was the wife of Ananias? *(Sapphira)*
13. Who was the wife of Aquila? *(Priscilla)*
14. Who was the wife of Zacharias? *(Elisabeth)*

Date used _____

Group_____

Response _____

Bible Authors

1. What Bible author led the Israelites to the promised land? *(Moses)*
2. What Bible author anointed the first kings of Israel? *(Samuel)*
3. What Bible author prayed for wisdom above all else? *(Solomon)*
4. What Bible author was swallowed by a big fish? *(Jonah)*
5. What Bible author commanded the Israelite armies in their conquest of the promised land? *(Joshua)*
6. What Bible author saw a vision of wheels? *(Ezekiel)*
7. What Bible author was cast into a den of lions? *(Daniel)*
8. What Bible author saw seraphim crying, "Holy, holy, holy"? *(Isaiah)*
9. What Bible author is known as the weeping prophet? *(Jeremiah)*
10. What Bible author was a shepherd, a musician and a king? *(David)*
11. What Bible author was cupbearer to a king? *(Nehemiah)*
12. What Bible author was a physician? *(Luke)*
13. What Bible author was a Pharisee? *(Paul)*
14. What two Bible authors were fishermen? *(Peter and John)*
15. What Bible author was a tax collector? *(Matthew)*
16. What Bible author was a scribe and priest? *(Ezra)*

Date used _____

Group_____

Response _____

Numbers (10 or below)

(Answers to these questions can be shown by holding up the proper number of fingers. Or use any of the games at the beginning of this quiz section.)

1. In how many days did God make the world? *(6)*
2. How many days was Jesus in the tomb? *(3)*
3. How many days was Lazarus dead? *(4)*
4. How many persons in the Trinity? *(3)*
5. How many true Gods? *(1)*
6. How many men thrown in the fiery furnace? *(3)*
7. How many commandments written in stone? *(10)*
8. How many great commandments in the New Testament? *(2)*
9. How many tribes in the northern kindgom? *(10)*
10. How many tribes in the southern kingdom? *(2)*
11. How many Gospels? *(4)*
12. How many books of Moses? *(5)*
13. How many books of poetry? *(5)*
14. How many books of major prophets? *(5)*
15. How many New Testament books of history? *(1)*
16. How many people saved in the ark? *(8)*

Date used _____

Group_____

Response _____

Numbers (over 10)

1. How many books in the New Testament? *(27)*
2. How many books in the Old Testament? *(39)*
3. How many books in the Bible? *(66)*
4. How many Old Testament books of history? *(12)*
5. How many books of minor prophets? *(12)*
6. How many were in the house of Jacob when he traveled to Egypt? *(70)*
7. How many tribes of Israel? *(12)*
8. How many years did the nation live in Egypt? *(430)*
9. How many Israelite men when the nation finally left Egypt? *(600,000)*
10. How many years in the wilderness? *(40)*
11. How many years of captivity? *(70)*
12. How many men in Gideon's army? *(300)*
13. How many prophets of Baal on Mount Carmel? *(450)*
14. How many men did Jesus feed from 5 loaves and 2 fishes? *(5,000)*
15. How many men did Jesus feed from 7 loaves and a few fishes? *(4,000)*
16. How many times should we forgive? *(70 x 7, every time)*

Date used _____

Group_____

Response _____

When Did It Happen? (Series I)

Three important periods of Israel's history are the periods of:

1. the patriarchs.
2. the wanderings.
3. dwelling in the land.

Tell which period each event or item belongs to. The players may all answer by raising one, two, or three fingers. Or you may play one of the games given at the beginning of this quiz section. The three periods may be written on the chalkboard.

Call of Abraham *(1)*   The brass serpent *(2)*
Building the tabernacle *(2)*   Saul chasing David *(3)*
Jacob's ladder *(1)*   Gideon's 300 men *(3)*
Building the temple *(3)*   Water from the rock *(2)*
David killing Goliath *(3)*   The bowl of pottage *(1)*
Jacob working for Rachel *(1)*   Manna *(2)*
Offering of Isaac *(1)*   Queen of Sheba *(3)*
The ten commandments *(2)*   Sodom destroyed *(1)*

Date used _____

Group_____

Response _____

When Did It Happen? (Series II)

While Israel was in the land the time may be divided into three periods, as follows:

1. Joshua and the conquest.
2. Judges.
3. Kings.

Tell which period each event or item belongs to. The players may all answer by raising one, two, or three fingers. Or you may play one of the games given at the beginning of this quiz section. The three periods may be written on the chalkboard.

Walls of Jericho *(1)*
Riddle of the lion and the honey *(2)*
Achan and the loot from Ai *(1)*
Jonathan and the arrows *(3)*
Solomon the wisest man *(3)*
Samson the strongest man *(2)*
Sun and moon stand still *(1)*
Shadow on sundial moves backward *(3)*
Rahab and the red cord *(1)*
Samuel anoints David *(3)*
Deborah's song *(2)*
The sign of the fleece *(2)*
David sins *(3)*
Contest on Mount Carmel *(3)*
Crossing the Jordan on a dry path *(1)*
Elijah and the chariot of fire *(3)*

Date used _____

Group_____

Response _____

The Old World or the New?

The old world stood before the flood, and the world that is now came after the flood. Tell whether each of these items or people belong:

(1) before the flood.
(2) after the flood.

All players may answer by raising their left hands for 1 and their right hands for 2. Or use one of the games given at the beginning of this quiz section. It would be good to write "Before the flood" on the chalkboard at the children's left and "After the flood" at the children's right.

Creation of the world	*(1)*	Adam sinned	*(1)*
Tower of Babel	*(2)*	Noah's sons settled the earth	*(2)*
Kingdom of Solomon	*(2)*	Adam's sons and daughters settled the earth	*(1)*
Garden of Eden	*(1)*	God rested on the seventh day	*(1)*
Call of Abraham	*(2)*	God commanded that we keep the Sabbath	*(2)*
Cain killed Abel	*(1)*	Methuselah, the oldest man	*(1)*
David killed Goliath	*(2)*	Noah built the ark	*(1)*
The ten commandments	*(2)*	Enoch walked with God	*(1)*

Date used _____

Group_____

Response _____

Christmas

(T—True   F—False   O—We don't know)

1. Many Old Testament prophecies told that Jesus would come. *(T)*
2. An angel announced to Mary that Jesus would be born. *(T)*
3. An angel announced to Joseph that Jesus would be born. *(T)*
4. Joseph and Mary traveled to Jerusalem just before the birth of Jesus. *(F)*
5. Mary rode on a donkey. *(O)*
6. Jesus was born in a stable in Bethlehem. *(T)*
7. Jesus is the son of Joseph *(F)*
8. Jesus is the Son of God. *(T)*
9. Angels announced to some shepherds that Jesus was born. *(T)*
10. The shepherds followed the star to find Jesus. *(F)*
11. Wise men followed the star to find Jesus. *(T)*
12. There were three wise men. *(O)*
13. There were three shepherds. *(O)*
14. The shepherds saw Jesus wrapped in swaddling clothes, lying in a manger. *(T)*
15. The wise men worshiped baby Jesus as He lay in a manger. *(F)*
16. The wise men traveled on camels. *(O)*

Date used _____

Group_____

Response _____

DATE DUE			
OCT 17 '83			
JAN 22 1988			
12/16/88			
1/6/88			
Oct 24 1989			
NOV 19 1990			
10/5/91			
7/17/92			
ILL 59984			
5-13-94			
# 32 29246			
#0/09/94			
APR 2 1 1998			
10/98			
APR 2 4 2001			

HIGHSMITH 45-102   PRINTED IN U.S.A.

1. _____ and be raised

2. _____

3. _____ they could each

4. _____ npanied Jesus'

5. _____ d before. *(T)*
6. _____ day. *(T)*
7. _____ the tomb. *(F)*
8. _____ ey slept instead

9. _____ d God's plan. *(F)*
10. _____ us would die for

11. _____
12. _____ e from the dead.

13. _____ ins forgiven. *(T)*
14. All who believe on Jesus will be raised from the dead. *(T)*

Date used _____

Group_____

Response _____

74051